she falls again

she falls again

poetry by
rosanna deerchild

illustrations by
mary mooswa

Coach House Books, Toronto

first edition

Published with the generous assistance of the Canada Council for the Arts and the
Ontario Arts Council. Coach House Books also acknowledges the support of the
Government of Canada through the Canada Book Fund and the Government of Ontario
through the Ontario Book Publishing Tax Credit.

LIBRARY AND ARCHIVES CANADA CATALOGUING IN PUBLICATION

Title: She falls again / poetry by Rosanna Deerchild ; illustrations by Mary Mooswa.
Names: Deerchild, Rosanna, author. | Mooswa, Mary, illustrator.
Identifiers: Canadiana (print) 20240433890 | Canadiana (ebook) 20240436997 | ISBN
9781552454879 (softcover) | ISBN 9781770568334 (EPUB) | ISBN 9781770568341
(PDF)
Subjects: LCGFT: Poetry.
Classification: LCC PS8607.E445 S54 2024 | DDC C811/.6—dc23

She Falls Again is available as an ebook: ISBN 978 1 77056 833 4 (EPUB), ISBN 978 1
77056 834 1 (PDF)

Purchase of the print version of this book entitles you to a free digital copy. To claim
your ebook of this title, please email sales@chbooks.com with proof of purchase. (Coach
House Books reserves the right to terminate the free digital download offer at any time.)

I offer this up for all our sisters who are lost.
And to honour all the many who refuse to stop searching.
Until all of our women have been returned home.

table of contents

insanity is just a number

i'm insane
there i said it
i am insane

no you're not

the crow flips around the branch like a child on the
monkey bars

yup, i'm insane

it's not a big deal you know
lots of people talk to animals
in fact all your people did

maybe but most animals don't usually talk back

sure they do

the crow coos and hops off the branch
flips its wings out
lands gracefully in front of me

the problem is
people just don't listen

stretches one stick thin leg at a time

actually it's quite clichéd
talking crow
indians
regular old cultural storytelling stuff really

(11)

it's been done a million times in a million stories
and no offence but it's been done way better
i mean a poet losing her mind in a park
talking to trickster   please

trickster   you say
really
right okay
let's go with that

why are you here trickster

   i'm getting to that anyways sometimes
   we gotta speak your clumsy language
   to get our point across

so do you have a point
or a cross

   i don't think i like your tone missy
   here i am taking time out of my daydream to talk to you

   have some respeck

      crow peck-pecks at the ground

fine
i can't believe i'm having this conversation
instead of running and screaming like a normal person

     crow loves this
     he laughs for a good ten minutes
     flapping his wings and shuck-shucking
     stupid bird

finally stops and clears throat

i have a message for you

what is it

i imagine people see me talking to a crow
mutter: poor insane girl

are you sure you wanna know
what crow knows

the black bird shuffles like a two-step jigger

i mean insanity and all

cocks head sideways

well you may as well
i don't have anything else to do today
except go insane

short trip eh
cawcawcaccaaaaw

the crow laughs for another ten minutes

seriously

okay okay
here's the message
well it's more of a story
in fact
it's exactly a story

sigh

stop me if you've heard this one
it's about The Woman Who Falls From The Sky

stop i've heard this one

ssssssshhhhh
pay attention
it's about The Woman Who Falls From The Sky

leans in close
again

the crow looks around back and forth

and she is pissed

undone drum

dreamed of a drum
saving mission

old woman
put her in my hands

dry and cracked
how do i save her

bathe her in water
she is thirsty

feast her with berries
she is hungry

sing honour songs
back into her sound

gently carry
her broken notes

my unsteady voice
my unsure hands

cannot recall
the drum songs

cannot hold
her notes together

i am an empty belly
a desert mouth

her skin
loosens from her frame

bindings unravel
beats scatter

she becomes   undone

good-skin woman

she has granite-smooth skin
unfailing hands

heartbeat
a defiant drum

bones too strong to break
she is good-skin woman

i am one hundred years
away from her

in just-surviving skin
this too heavy i want to leave

on a hook abandon in a bar skin
because this brown is a bull's-eye skin

i am one hundred honour songs
away from her

my fearful heartbeat
a scared rabbit just before the snare

i am one hundred ceremonies
away from her

digging deep
in my bone memory

for a drum song
that will get me close to her

i pick and pull
at this loose skin

try to make it fit
make it granite-smooth skin

indian heart

keep my indian heart
in a mason jar

nestled in cedar
sage and sweetgrass

it's red tobacco tie
        a prayer

waiting

for a ceremony
to set her free

in the shape of a country

genevieve died of tuberculosis
at clearwater lake indian hospital

buried in an unmarked grave
no one knows where exactly

her daughters
ripped and stripped

from homeland
kin the colour of their skin

taken to guy hill indian residential school
in the same goddamn place

elijah died on his trapline
where his family survived one season at a time

when she was just born
whispered edna

with his last breath
his only gift for his baby girl

sometimes
mama tells me

she imagines genevieve
escaped the sanatorium

ran away
maybe to winnipeg

or all the way to france
took her french name

became a famous jazz singer
her heartbreak songs

all in Cree
all about her lost girls

papa bruce was a music man
who ran away

and left a space in the shape
of a hank williams song

i imagine his lonesome songs
all in the shape of me

his Cree mother
a matriarch

a medicine woman
anna stands razor straight

eyes pierce even in fuzzy
black and white pictures

his father served in the war
his handsome face

his blue eyes reflect
his scottish fur-trading ancestor

before going to war
stanley traded fur like his father

sent from Pimicikamak to Wînipêk
to bramshott and shorncliffe

remade a little black devil
sent back home broken

mustard gas nightmares
and influenza lungs

my family bears scars
in the shape of a country

but my roots are deeper

endless growth
that goes all the way

back to before
this place was cut

into the shape
of oh canada

our home
on native land

i got indian credentials

drink water out of jars
all sizes

mason jars   pickle jars
spaghetti   peanut butter   jam
even those fancy classico's
i got the whole damn set
i don't discriminate

my cupboards crowded
with margarine containers
they are indian tupperware
mismatched mugs   chipped and worn
dollar store cutlery   mixed with fancy ones
individually wrapped when they were bought

i know every hank williams song ever written
senior and junior
the lyrics are stick and poke
tattooed on my heart

the voices
of my mother
her mother and hers
carry in my blood and bone
not in my pocket
not written in a resume
only pulled out
for speeches and accolades

my father is in a long line of men
who left me

it stretches
all the way
back to world war one

i have never been mistaken
for anything
but brown indian squaw
bush native status too rezzie not rezzie enough
first nations aboriginal and/or indigenous

i have been
employed unemployed
well off dirt poor homeless drunk sober
ceremonial religious and/or in between gods

i have been told
to shut up more times than i can count
keep secrets wear a skirt sit
in the back keep your head
down do your job
don't do your job you're too loud
too opinionated too difficult
too much not enough

i am more likely to be assaulted
abused ignored blamed shamed
taken
and/or killed

many times all at once
this is a burden i will carry all my life

i don't speak Cree but the rhythm carries
me back to bone memory

boreal forest
thick wild rivers
the winter resting place
O-pipon-na-piwin
ᐅᐱᐳᓇᐱᐄᑐ

until hydro
drowned us out

i don't pow wow   no coordination
no tribal tattoos   too painful a reminder
gifted a drum   a feather
but do not play or pray
on the pedestal of social opinion

my heartbeat joins the beat of a thousand ancestors
without interruption   without interpretation   without missing a beat

someday i will find the bones of my grandmother
and bring them home

someday i will find the grave of my grandfather
and leave tobacco

these stories are scars i turn to stars
set free in the sky of telling

this is my story
and no one else's

i got a christmas hamper from my nation

inside
a frozen bird with one leg missing
one can of no-name cranberry sauce
a box of instant potatoes tang crystals
one can of cream corn and package gravy

inside
a humble feast in a cardboard box
more precious than a manger

inside
a community that claims you
in its offering

inside
a gift
that says you belong here

the ark

okay okay

stutters crow

have you heard this one
the world is ending
all the leaders have a biiiiig meeting to make the decision of
all decisions
countries combine resources to build an enormous spaceship
they name it the ark

seriously
bit on the nose isn't it

hey   are you writing this story or is crow

wait   what

ahem ... where was i
ah yes
scientists gather the world's dna from ants to zebras
seeds from every plant life are stored
they figure out how to make water
a small atmosphere
a tiny forest that gives off a thousand times more oxygen

as for humans – well – there's only one strict rule
only people in love are allowed on the ark
true love
a one in a million chance right
slimmer than a government promise

because it's not the warriors or the rule makers
it's the lovers who will save us all

the end is near

sounds familiar

are you sure

crow shuffles toward me

yeah i think i saw that movie on netflix

i sigh hoping this bird gets on with pecking my eyes out

you were saying something
about the woman who fell out of the sky
and a message

falls   she falls
again
but yeah   sure sure

shuffles in a little closer

i mean we still got time right
it's not like the polar ice caps are melting

and crow laughs until he cries

rising moon

this is the story
of how this happens

you name us whales
a puny weak word
as though you have the right
of creator

for millennia we were silent
        going about our business
        we never bothered you
the two-legs-who-walk-above are a mystery to us
the slow currents of our lives   too big

for you to understand
our wise ancient language can
not cross the border between us   we are separate
but like the great mother herself
we are halves of a circle
unbroken   balanced   until now

the two-legs-who-walk-above are too many
        always spilling down
        into our world clumsy and awkward
        arrogant   sharp splinters of broken shells

harpoons tear into our ageless families ripping them apart
once those tools were carried by those-who-live-in-harmony
our old ones saw comfort in its end
    now they bring only pain and death

our waters are poison
the old ones say those-that-walk-above cut her open
drain her of life

at first we didn't believe it
who would do such a thing
it was madness

then we saw with our own eyes
the dark beast crawls on its belly
its insatiable hunger never satisfied

the babies start dying
all the time the mother's mourning song can be heard
  through the waters
   a song heard only once or twice in a generation

now if you listen
you can always hear the long sad wail
of a mother's broken heart through the deep

it is the time of the great famine
salmon are coming less and less
there is not enough for everyone
still our mothers bear the next generations

a young one has her first calf
she is so happy so proud
she names him rising moon
to honour the wax and wane
the coming and going of the tides and flow of currents
the intertwining of these things

it is a good name
but rising moon dies
his mother's grief cannot be contained
not in her heart
not in the four days of the death ceremony
not in her mourning song
not even by the ocean itself

instead she gathers all her grief
     her vengeance   her rage
     into the medicine bundle of her belly and rises
     just like her baby's name she becomes a full moon rising
through the dark blue of the sea upward upward upward

she carries rising moon to the surface
she carries him to the very edge
holds him up to the two-legs
cries *here* *see what you have done*

she begs for mercy
for many nights lingers there
swims many miles   carrying the carcass of her first born like a beacon
                a warning

but you are not moved

     still you bring the great beast through
     still you slow the salmon   the spawning rivers are empty
     still you come

the water nations gather
the old ones say

something must be done
we must teach these tiny fragile beings
we must guide them

the young mothers speak
they kill our children
starve us
steal our salmon
something must be done

the warrior ones agree
something must be done
we grow tired
we are fewer every spawn
we must fight back

so we fight   we resist   we attack your great canoes

break our fins against your rudders
ram our very bodies against the hardness of your hearts

all the while hoping
you will see us
you will finally know that we are connected
you must make treaty with us

just as the rising moon
over the ocean

a prayer for mistâpêw

i pray they never find you
just what you leave behind

fish bones in tangled hair
carelessly left
big foot along beach

lost   perhaps   while on a stroll
with sasquatch nichimos

a blurry picture
taken at midnight
in a nebraska campground

snapped while going to the bathroom
scaring the shit out of hunters

a dark moving smudge
on the impossible slope
of a snowy mountain

a ski trip with your reclusive cousin
yeti who you visit once a year

big brother   always stay elusive
always just vanish over horizon
never stay still for face pullers

until sightings are a thing of the past
a myth   a lie proven scientifically impossible

forgive us our trespass
on your sacred kingdoms
mistâpêw   i offer this ciscêmâs

may you never be discovered
uncovered poked and prodded

trapped in a box labelled conquered
may your name always be whispered in secret

mistâpêw stay
forever hallowed
forever sacred
forever free

even the sky was angry

its blustery wind
its dark clouds

that day in Maskwacis
the pope came

with his sorry
his tour of penitence

his prayers loud across
our lands

crowned
with eagle feather bonnet

while the bones
of our children still

lie silent
in schoolyard graves

if only
they had told him

each barb on each feather
a child you have taken

each feathery down
a child you have lost

would he know then
the true weight of our grief

would he know then
the true weight of this truth

if only
they had whispered

in the pope's ear
francis

this headdress is not a gift
this headdress is a treaty

a promise that you will
do no more harm

fallen monuments

i have no space to grieve for your fallen monuments
i am still mourning the children buried in the ground

i have no strength for shaming those who felled the queen
i am using it to hold the bodies of my sisters

i have no tears for your statues toppled on stolen lands
they are as hollow as your promises

history mementos

it is written on my mother's residential school skin
it is whispered by my grandmother's tb ghost
it is the lonely grave of my grandfather in your field of honour
it is the target on my back

that says missing and murdered while still alive
there are no statues of us   no commemoration
    only erasure
    only the blank pages of your history books you never bother to learn

cigar store indian

what do we have here
you ask yourself

easy settler smile
colonizer reach

fawning gasp
how lovely gaze past

my blockade
body language

your callused thumb
grazes my earlobe

cool fingers
fondle my beads

slowly caress
my braid

whisper *marvellous*
take it all in

before you disappear
down the ethnic food

aisle at the grocery store
i am left standing stunned

just a cigar store indian
for you to consume

indian summer

on the corner
waiting to pass go

precarious
on a wedge of concrete

she strides up bold
declares *what a beautiful day*

sure is   i muse
must be indian summer   she replies

i slide over the squintiest of auntie-side-eyes
slip closer to the curb

she throws up her stop sign hands
well that's what we grew up with

i'm Métis   her light skin shining
        and i'm not offended
        no one should be

cautions admonishment

my heart races cars
racing by cutting the air

anyway   she yells red
YOU PEOPLE KEEP CHANGING THE WORDS

push the cross button
again again again

push myself
away from her

away from her fast moving words
away from my silence

they impact – crash   debris   everywhere

in the shade of my skin

almost racist
he said on the thin blue line
not all the way racist
because that would be
unacceptable

almost racist   don't forget the air quotes
'almost racist'   we don't want it to get away
'almost racist'   as in it's not really racist

excuse me   he interjects
it's overtones
not undertones
we decide how much tone
we're the tone police

he insists
'almost racist'
but just on the surface
because we don't dig deep
enough to dig out
the root

he judges
those people always jump
at shadows everyone knows
only shadows are really racist

those shady characters doing shady things
in the shade   in case my case wasn't clear
clears throat *ahem ahem ahem*

anyway those people don't know anything
until we tell them to know
what to know and when to know it
in the never-ending inquiry of all things to know
which we run too by the way

anyway he concludes everyone knows
it's all just a matter of shade

blurring indians

under the mainstreet bridge
medicine wheels
turn to targets
graffiti arrows
hunt remnants of buffalo
surrounded by white
concrete
constant
tumbleweed of traffic
blurring indians
all the way down
stripped to bone
by the sharp teeth of progress
their deaths on display
during rush hour traffic
over and over again

valentine

indian street love
carries his broken heart

in a blue walmart bag
an unopened gift

loud and limping lament
it was all for her

lost my soulmate
it's all my fault

wails wet words
sloppy tears

floods a heartbreak poem
all the way down

rush hour sidewalk

rush

before she was gone
in the skywalk

over donald and graham
valentine held his heart

can you play us a song
drops a loonie in a busker's guitar case

a slow one says heart-woman
nestled against his chest

guitar man strums garth brooks
lookin back at the memory

of the dance we shared
indian street love waltzes

real slow
right there in the skywalk

over donald and graham
he held her

among bustling crowds
pushing past

above waves of cars
rushing below

before she was
swept away

just for a heartbeat
valentine had dreams

rules for urban indians

when they ask
can i help you find something

they don't mean
can i help you
find something

they mean
can i help you find
the door

shuffle you out like a bad
julia roberts movie

learn to hold body
in such a way

straight back
no nonsense

resting auntie face
from a thousand years back

keep hands out of pockets
bags closed tight

eyes straight
do not stray

stay inside the lines
of their suspicion

stare down security guard
with treaty making glare

till you make it out the door
but that don't mean

let your guard down
because you still gotta

watch your back
do not make eye contact

with those white boys
in the slow moving truck

trying to catch
your eye like a hook

walk inside a run
as they crawl by

strike your fist up hard
full of fuck off

as they flip you off
screech down the street

squawuglybitch
didntwantcha anyway

whisper *kinanâskomitinâwâw*
to the ancestors

because they only say
it's a good day to die in the movies

at portage place first nation

indians greet each other
with secret sacred head nod

Tansi
Aniin
Wachay

noisy birds
forever circling

forever searching for home
on their own homeland

at portage place
first nation

hickeys are love potion
they tell people you're tooken

bead work is bead bling
the bigger the better

and revolutions happen
in a round dance

wanted

professional protester
to put body on line
between pipe and land

duties include
blockade construction
land and water defence
angry settler offence

may get shot at and/or run over
arrested and/or attacked

no wage
no benefits
no privileges

must bring own bandanas
army fatigues
and eagle feathers

apply within

side effects include: government surveillance
public ridicule, jail time, and complex post-colonization stress disorder
justice not included

revolution
at portage place first nation

security guards
guard the goods

for the good people
who've paid

for the constitutional
right to shop there

stop the people
who've come

for some round
dance justice

mall cops with badges
flash-crash false power

over little old men
whose only crime

is to sit on a sign
that says do not sit here

get out get they shout
rosa parks him out

have your revolution
elsewhere

back in dodge
the federation of cowboys

who hate indians
claim victory

in the public square
in the public interest

shoot off mouths
like six-shooter guns

save our
taxpayer dollahs

hollahs praise
the law

can i get an ahhmen

and down
on the front line

police pull
apart our circles

line up
their usual suspects

put your hands
in the air

they shout
drop your eagle feathers

while we check
for illegal hand drums

guns drawn
on our bodies

later headlines
will play a blame game

thug-shots ring out
louder than the truth

interrupt this regularly
scheduled program

for federal indian agent
who comes to town

to flash-crash
indian-boss badge

decree the latest
indian-act-law

indians must
become

more transparent
until invisible

must trade treaties
for perpetual negotiations

no discussion
no excuses

no exception
no problem

sign here
sign there

sign all your
asse(t)s goodbye

shake hands
snap pictures

smile
in reconciliation

they keep telling us
resistance is futile

we keep telling them
resistance is all we know

they push with guns
while our people stand with feathers

they call us savage
while they ravage

the earth our mother
sneak the black snake

through her veins
oil stains we can't wash out

but still we dance at the crossroads
still we raise our fists and resist

the woman who falls from the sky — again

there i was minding my own business   mostly
when this woman falls from the sky
tapwe   tapwe
true story
knocked me right off my feet   that one
right there in the middle of the street
right there in the middle of the afternoon
that's not even the half of it
cheskwa
just wait

the-woman-who-falls-from-the-sky was an indian woman
sure   it was unmistakable
brown skin
long black hair
cheek bones that cut
looking madder than a broken treaty

well just as the crow flies i decide the best approach is a direct one
hey big sister   i says   is the sky falling
brush-brush my wounded shoulder and smile

the woman-who-falls-from-the-sky
right in the middle of the road
right in the middle of the day
says   i am the only begotten daughter

can you believe that
Tapwe

well you sure don't look like a deity
and crow knows a thing or two about that   let me tell you

that entrance for starters
you can't just fall out of the sky and land on crow
what do i look like – a turtle
besides it's rude
i should know
in fact being rude might be the one thing i do know

truth be told   i felt a little ripped off
all the others got burning bushes
lights descending
visions
miracles
even a stone tablet that one time   two of them   even
all i got was whiplash
no thunder   not even lightning
this one wasn't even glowing   pssh
anyways

i asks her   is it the end already
scratch-scratch my head
i always hoped i would be here for this

falls-from-the-sky
says   no   it's the beginning

oh ho i says and rub my wings together
now we'll see some tricks

no   no   she-who-falls says
i do not walk on water or turn it into wine
water is sacred   water is life   not for cheap tricks
if you ask me my brother is a bit of a show-off
and so dramatic   i mean a cross really jesus

admittedly i was disappointed
but enthralled nonetheless
it's not every millennium when such a powerful family will confess
and i did feel bad for her
what with all that falling
and she didn't even have any shoes
i figure maybe she needs a foot wash
so   what are you doing here then
i says to her while eyeing her feet

falling-again says
i am here to start the revolution

whuuu … whuu i told her
settle down
last time that happened so many of the people died
it flipped everything upside down
flip flop
don't get crazy now
i say with a flap of wide wings
boy i'll never say that again

fallen-woman whomped me on the head with her giant turtle medallion
thuck thuck   just like that
oh you trickster better listen to me, she says
i won't have any of your bullshit this time

language   language
i smart talk back
rub-rub my head

as you wish, she smiles and repeats herself in Nêhiyawêwin
then in Anishinaabemowin
then Inuktitut

then all the original tongues
fall like a rainstorm

okay okay i get it
what do you want from me
a humble crow
and bow real low just like they do in disney cartoons

well   let me tell you   one should never ask that question
unless you want the answer to kick you right in the ass
just like they do in disney cartoons

she-who-falls-the-world leans in real close like and says
i want you to deliver the message

gravity

sister astronaut told me

it's not the falling
from the sky

you have to worry about
it's the landing

star maps

sister astronomer told me

man is the only species
that builds cities

then gets lost in them
he simply stopped

asking the stars
for directions

gospel according to crow

on the corner of arlington
and bannerman where

a cartoon jesus stretches
his arms out wide

i save a one-legged crow
from a one-eyed cat

crow peg-leg stumbles
over curb falls head over wing

one-eyed cat stalks
low and quick

rescued just
before the leap

crow gifts me
a ceremony

or maybe
a curse

laughs long and throaty
in on the joke

does a one-legged
grass dance

under cathedral
of north end trees

spreads wings out wide
smudges me down

with the smoke
exhaust of passing cars

cawcawcaws
gospel according to crow

even
a one legged crow

even
a scavenger like me

even
a not even crow

can be sacred
enough to save

wînipêk

frail elm tree fingers
splay open

in winter
in summer

fists of leaves
rise to sky

dirty water city
broken and held together

by railroad
stitches and band-aid bridges

divide north and south
trains wail long and lonesome

always leave
always come back

her street light smiles
brighter than stars here

her downtown tattoos
tell dirty jokes

flash flashes her
main street raincoat

wild skin scarred
by concrete colonization

her telltale heart is buried deep
under the barriers of portage and main

unheard in the roar
of this settler story

her story stumbles along
narrow avenues

whisper slides down
side streets

graffiti secrets
scrawled on walls

she says

i am here
i am here
i am here

a circle

of teenagers stand
outside their north end
high school smudge
under grey sky

a circle
of crows fly overhead
stitches of arrows
pierce the rising smoke

the big drum

outside my window heard
the slow steady beat of a big drum

but it was just an indian girl
wearing too big boots

scuffling her own rhythmic beat
along a cracked sidewalk

a ragged beat reverberating
lingering for blocks

north end barbies on the boulevard

two teen girls strut by
two different shades of brown skin

two different shades of pink barbie wigs
two shimmering jewels in the sun

north end boys

ride their bikes
no reflectors

dark hoodies
hands free

dark silhouettes
glide soundlessly

remind
me of centaurs

these sentries
in the night

there are no indians

only murder
of crows here

left to criss-cross
last rites

over street-light crucifixes
lining north end streets

drawn by gang lines
police do-not-cross

lines and body outlines
sprawling urban legends

here in this
wild-wild-west show

night ladies
are laid out

played out
like card games

queens sold out
in some back alley

trade between suburban
cowboys and crime story indians

down on main street
gods and girls

sell salvation
to passing cars

make neon promises
of love love love

lies lies lies
along her body

a constellation
of scars

forgotten stars
long burned out

by siren screams
down throat

a nation with no tongues
lost in translation

a bastardization
of duncan c scott's

poetic ending: to absorb
into the mainstream nation

every indian
until there is

no problem
no question

his unsettling solution
this unsettling of skins

a murder of crows

covers naked tree
along river vein

flood ravaged
stripped of life

still her arms
reach for sun

hold a bundle
of crow a burst

of dark notes
all at once

cawcawcaw
dance on limbs

a ragged cacophony
of crow choir

calls in each day
in dirty water city

a mourning song
echoes

bothersome

how they keep showing up

in bins back lanes
along roadsides

always digging
secrets up

nothing stays buried
now

am i talking crow
or am i talking girl

hard to tell here
sometimes

dark hair
like feathers

fallen

fragile wings
broken

weather bleached
bones

splayed wing tips
reaching

upward
toward the sun

in the mother hood

hood mothers
gather at selkirk and powers
dance at portage and main
stand with arm raised
against citadels of power

some less
mother than warrior
mourning
another fallen son
another stolen sister

lost on too many streets
graffiti headstones
line too many
alleyways here

taken from too many corners
to sell soul for crack pipe dreams
spills into nightmare

lost but not lost

not like how you lose
your keys
or your way
or your place

because people always look
for those things

in the mother hood

hood mothers
don't blink
must keep eyes
peeled for gang flash
flashing police cars pass

skin traders troll
slow along sidewalk
past park slide by school
hunt for young brown skin

hood mothers
swear shake fists
pray those cops cruise by
peek through blinds to see
where they will stop

watch which mother
will be less today

here in the mother hood

missing is a name

they don't even bother
to know us just number us

list us shuffle us
around crowded desks
pin-up girls on bulletin boards
wrap us around lamp posts

make us small
square pictures
like stamp collections

sent to lie
in silent stacks
rows of faces
with no voices

they don't even bother
to look for us

we are not
missing
just not here

but where
we have gone
they cannot say

we are not dead
we are the body

this country lies on
our highway of tears

fill sea to sea
but they don't see

they don't even bother
to bury us just stuff us
in boxes marked out
leave us in trash
ditch us in field
dump us in back alley

they don't even bother
to mourn us

we are just
another crime
another statistic
another number

our name is 1,181
little
2 little
3 little indian squaws
and this number
should offend you more than this word
because the count keeps growing

they don't even bother
to explain why so many
of just-us go without justice
just tell us

justice is a privilege
we do not deserve

no room
no justice
no peace

because we are the kind of girl
who does not even exist

we are just

indian woman
faded black and white

whispers of a long gone past
like horses and fur trading

we are just
your disney porn

girl who wears feathers
dances barefoot across

your screen before inviting
you into our tipis

we are just
a decoration

a symbol if his story
rides into sunset

slips between sheets
of your status quo

we are just
a body of land conquered

cut squares labelled sold off
a resource extraction

oh but i know
another story

her story
a strong woman song

her recall of ancestors
that go back millennia

she is older than
your confederation

your declaration
that we are not here

in this place
you keep trying to take

but our roots
go deeper

than your fingers
your lashing tongue

your machine
called patriarchy

we are
the matriarchy

herstory is earth
where you stand

she is the water
your beginning

she is our heart
beat

a re-creation story
that begins

with
a whisper

calling all her names
back

a drum song
rising thrum thrum

thrumming
of heart beats

a rising
that begins

with

one

voice

rising

my voice
rising

with my
sisters

rising

with my
mother
rising
for my daughters

a rising
my name is
sacred

my name is
Iskwew

my name
my name
my name

is not missing

crazy not insane, or do i have that backwards

start with the poets
they're crazy anyway

hey
what are you saying

what what
everyone says that
who in their right mind
wants to be a poet when they grow up

what's that supposed to mean

stop interrupting

crow scolds while wagging its wing tip like a fingertip

where was i   ah yes   the poets

all right   i says to falls-from-the-sky   start with the poets
but – I ask her – what am i starting
i'm really good at starting things
just tell me who needs a good lesson
i says it's my specialty

she-falls-again says to me
stop interrupting

so crow stands on his head just to mix things up

okay okay i'm listening

start with the poets
but only the women
because let's face it
the men are too busy
comparing the size of their stanzas

yes i shout at her and laugh
for a generation or two
you can't beat a good long prose
start with the women poets
she-fell-in continues without missing a beat

those ones who speak this sacred text
who pass on the secrets to their daughters
in the lullaby and drum of their hearts
and who whisper it to theirs

tell her
tell her
tell herstory

she sings retribution

my existence is a resistance
my body a movement

settlers can't settle down
this wild brown woman

my red dress is no redress
this ragged dress

is this this country's flag
this red maple leaf

your hand
over my mouth

barely able to hold
in my primal scream

my tight muscles
taut tendons

struggle to stay
in the lines

always
being pushed

in
the
margins

break through

going the wrong way
up your one-way

blocking up the highways
a long way

from reconciliation

uncover

we are needles
in a haystack

unfindable

no

we are haystacks
of needles

piles of them
laid out in your field

of view
thousands of burial mounds

sharp and waiting
glinting in the sun

unturned

under weeping sky
down by two rivers

her wide arms
hold us close

we drum dance
grieve and love

we sing
her names

no name
missed

no one
forgotten

no stone
unturned

until we bring them
all home

shift (treaty 5)

Iskwew walks up
to the lined-up men

in the arbour
taking turns talking

passing the mic
like a sacred pipe

she tells them
stop

women should be here
in front of the men

invites the women
to take their place

i witness
a shift

an interruption
an intervention

in the way it's always been done
in the steady flow of women

making their way back
to the front

making their way back
to lead

the old people say

we come from Acāhkosak
we are star people

our people
came through Keewatin

the going home star
in Pipon we slid

down a braid
on the big dipper's handle

together
we make the universe

i like that
origin better

than adam
and his rib

we are a spider, weaving

a web

obese with music and dance
wild and tame lovers

hysterical laughter life
tears and death

we are echoes
vibrating through strands

prismatic infinite
rhythm and rhyme

fragile filaments
gone in a breath

a web
woven over and over

in the language of Nipi

snow
on bare skin

invisible
breath

barely forms
before

melting
into sigh

rain
drops on leaves

water
drum song

loud beats
slides into silent

tongue of earth

frozen river
secrets

waiting
for ice to crack

a scream
she made

a jagged truth
she told

wild river
mouth open

face upward
the rush

of her honour song
of her lelelelee

clouds hum
her melody

all her names
whispered lullabies

all over sky

lingers
between

sleep and wake
stars and earth

sky woman
       are you falling
             or rising

when you forget (ceremony)

my girl
look in the water

you are
the centre of a ripple

always
beginning and ending

the reflection
of a thousand ancestors

moon (ceremony)

my girl
look up at the moon

remember
your own wholeness

together

spring (ceremony)

felt
a quickening
a waking storm

breath
like wind
on uncovered skin

a seed
a dandelion

ready to leap

let's put a moonlodge on every corner like starbucks

hold the tea we'll have cookies wine
and couches with moss cushions

sisters will come in
for free back rubs

restore tired feet rest
hands that hold up the world

while digging roots
sing about power

sister january speaks in poetry
reminds us who the hell we are

and ulali trills all the women
back into the sky

let's take the men out of menstruation
bros been there long enough

erase the words *can't* and *don't* and *no*
replace with *can* and *do* and *give* and *yes*

we'll sit cross-legged
open legs hips moving

our sacred selves
pulsating power

our period a new beginning
instead of a painful silence

let's create a feast for one another
we've been force-fed too many lies

we'll sing each other up
our voices entwining braids

howl at the moon wild
difficult and dangerous

our grandmothers
saying yes yes

my daughters

sing

play

be silent no more

drum

i hear the sound
of her drum

i hear
the sound of my drum

i hear the sound of my drum
playing one beat

at a time
for all time

i am an indian poem

a thousand women
stand behind me

hold
the bloodline

sing
the storyline

pass
the thin line

i am the returning voice
from the silence

the telling
story

of my mother
my grandmother
my great-grandmother

i breathe them all in
and poetry breathes me out

my poem is an indian woman

i will tell you everything
while others write our eulogy

erase us
scribble us in the margins

i will write us alive
loud in the wide open

sky

acknowledgements

To the warrior women who stand at the front lines, who work behind the lines, who tell the stories, and who keep demanding an end to the ongoing crisis of MMIWG.

My sister, Mary Mooswa, who creates such powerful art for my words. My friend Alex Wilson and her dad, Stan Wilson, who helped with the Cree.

My bestie, Kim Wheeler, for helping to get this manuscript to the right people at the right time.

My girls, Kaydance and Raven, you are my inspiration and guidance in all things.

My mother, you survived so much so I could be here.

Kinanâskomitinâwâw
Hay hay

Rosanna Deerchild (she/her) is Cree, from the community of O-Pipon-Na-Piwin Cree Nation.

She is the host of CBC Radio One's *Unreserved*, the radio space for Indigenous people. Her debut poetry collection, *this is a small northern town*, won the 2009 Aqua Books Lansdowne Prize for Poetry. Her second book, *calling down the sky*, is a collaboration with her mother, Edna Ferguson (née Moose), a Residential School survivor. Her first play, *The Secret to Good Tea*, was produced by the Royal MTC's mainstage for their 2022/23 season and will also be produced by the Grand Theatre in London, Ontario, and at the NAC Indigenous Theatre in Ottawa in the 2025/26 season.

Mary Mooswa is from the O-Pipon-Na-Piwin Cree Nation, located in Northern Manitoba, but grew up in the mining town of Lynn Lake, Manitoba. She now lives in Nova Scotia with her two children. She creates using many mediums, such as watercolour, ink, pencil, collage, and acrylics.

She graduated from the University of Manitoba with degrees in fine art and education. She teaches in Nova Scotia.

Her art work has been published in several publications, including *Contemporary Verse 2* and *Emboss Magazine*. She has been part exhibitions in Manitoba and Nova Scotia, and had the honour of creating art for her sister Rosanna Deerchild's three books of poetry.

Her work is an expression of her culture and belief that everything is interconnected, has spirit, and is sacred. The work is lifelike but at the same time dreamy. Art has always been her first language.

Typeset in Arno and Le Havre.

Printed at the Coach House on bpNichol Lane in Toronto, Ontario, on Zephyr Antique Laid paper, which was manufactured, acid-free, in Saint-Jérôme, Quebec, from second-growth forests. This book was printed with vegetable-based ink on a 1973 Heidelberg KORD offset litho press. Its pages were folded on a Baumfolder, gathered by hand, bound on a Sulby Auto-Minabinda, and trimmed on a Polar single-knife cutter.

Coach House is located in Toronto, which is on the traditional territory of many nations, including the Mississaugas of the Credit, the Anishnabeg, the Chippewa, the Haudenosaunee, and the Wendat peoples, and is now home to many diverse First Nations, Inuit, and Métis peoples. We acknowledge that Toronto is covered by Treaty 13 with the Mississaugas of the Credit. We are grateful to live and work on this land.

Edited by Jordan Abel
Cover art *Sky Woman* by Mary Mooswa
Interior art *Insanity Is Just a Number, The Ark, I'm Here to Start the Revolution,* and *Calling the Women Back* by Mary Mooswa
Cover and interior design by Crystal Sikma

Coach House Books
80 bpNichol Lane
Toronto ON M5S 3J4
Canada

mail@chbooks.com
www.chbooks.com